The ~~Ten,~~
Make That (Nine,)
Habits of Very
Organized People.
Make That Ten.

Also by Steve Martin

The ~~Ten,~~ Make That (Nine,) Habits of Very Organized People. Make That Ten.

the tweets of Steve Martin

GRAND CENTRAL
PUBLISHING

NEW YORK · BOSTON

BOOK AND COVER DESIGN BY MUCCA DESIGN
ILLUSTRATIONS BY SERGE BLOCH
COPYRIGHT © 2012 BY 40 SHARE PRODUCTIONS, INC.

GRAND CENTRAL PUBLISHING
Hachette Book Group
237 Park Avenue
New York, NY 10017
www.HachetteBookGroup.com

Printed in the United States of America
Binder's Code: RRD-C
First Edition: February 2012

10 9 8 7 6 5 4 3 2 1

GRAND CENTRAL PUBLISHING is a division of HACHETTE BOOK GROUP, INC.

The GRAND CENTRAL PUBLISHING name and logo
is a trademark of HACHETTE BOOK GROUP, INC.

The HACHETTE SPEAKERS BUREAU provides a wide range
of authors for speaking events. To find out more,
go to www.hachettespeakersbureau.com
or call (866) 376-6591.

The publisher is not responsible for websites (or their content)
that are not owned by the publisher.

ISBN: 978-1-455-51247-8

Library of Congress Control Number: 2011942817

INTRODUCTION

I STARTED TWEETING FOR PURELY COMMERCIAL REASONS. I realized that when I did a television show to promote a book or record, and that television show had an audience of, say, four million people, about four hundred of them rushed out to buy the book or record. I figured if I had a Twitter audience of four hundred thousand—an audience that was tuned into *me*—and I promoted a book, then four hundred thousand of them would rush out and buy my book. Instead, forty of them rushed out to buy my book.

However, I soon lost my interest in promoting through Twitter, other than casually, and got hooked on the comedy potential. I found the limits exciting, and liked that these thoughts popped up randomly on someone else's *device*, perhaps catching them at an odd moment. I also liked that these thoughts popped up randomly in me, and kept me on my comedy toes. I thought tweeting might be a way to cultivate lines and ideas for my new banjo stage show I am now touring with. It wasn't. All this tweet material turned out to be good for one thing only: tweeting.

When I started, around Labor Day of 2010, I didn't really understand the ins and outs of Twitter, and it wasn't till about four months later that I noticed that people were tweeting me back. Then, I started noticing how tuned-in and funny the responses were, and then a few months later I started saving the best of them (cut and pasted, by hand, by me) in a file. This was real enjoyment: I would run to my wife quoting someone's latest clever response, laughing hard.

In a sense, this book has a narrative. Even though I've jumbled the tweets around for structure, if the book is read in order, which no one will, you can watch me stumble, get wise, get responsive, go from longer consecutive story tweets to shorter self-contained ones. At first, a complaint from a reader ("too long," "too many," etc) would make me panic and sweat like I was a first-time comedian on an audition stage. I made a vow to make my tweets grammatically correct, so if I erred I felt I looked like a dolt. (This led to a regular tweet called "Get it Right Friday," where I corrected any errors throughout the week. "Get it Right Friday," by the way, always came on Thursday.)

Once, a beginner's gaffe made me the most nervous and panicked I ever was but led to one of my best tweets. On my banjo tour with the Steep Canyon Rangers, the fastest way to get reviews was to search Twitter for my name after a show, which I did. Then I realized I had inadvertently tweeted my name. I instantly figured that my Twitter audience would conclude that I was searching myself on Twitter, highly embarrassing. After palpitations and perspirations, I composed myself and tweeted: "Steve Martin oily muscles beach Speedo photo." Then I immediately tweeted, "Sorry, meant to Google myself."

The ~~Ten,~~

Make That (Nine,)

Habits of Very

Organized People.

Make That Ten.

Kazowie! Kablooie! Hooboy!
Just mulling over some ideas
for celebrity baby names.

Going out today
to take pictures of paparazzi.

. . . .

Got some great pictures of paparazzi
today. Man, they UGLY! Went through
their garbage too. Found my own
garbage in their garbage.

. . . .

Been asked to appear
on the new primetime show,
"So You Think You Can Vomit."
Excited!

My publicist is nervous about my
becoming a Tweeter. He says celebrities
tend to make such monumental gaffes.
He's such a typical Wop!

The Red Cross is a really good cause,
but one billiard ball hitting another is
a really good cause and effect.

My wife doesn't know I'm Tweeting.
She thinks I'm writing a screenplay...

....

...So if you see me on the street, please
say, "How's the 'screenplay' going,
Steve?" We'll both do a "thumbs up"
and keep moving....

....

....

Could we have a rehearsal? Please say,
"How's the 'screenplay' going, Steve?"

....

Excellent. Don't over emphasize
"screenplay" because she's not stupid
and that would be a giveaway.
No winking either.

....

It's not
"How's the SCREENPLAY going?"
Bad. Amateur.

....

Remember, I'm a professional actor.
Let me do the heavy lifting.
Practice your thumbs up in front
of a mirror at home.

....

Some of you will make the mistake
of pointing your thumb down.
Don't worry.
A few tries will make it perfect.

....

Oh boy, lots of bad acting so far:

....

"How's the uh..uh..(look at palm)
SCREENPLAY going...uh..uh..(racking
brain) LESLIE NIELSEN." Yipes. Or:

....

"How's the screenplay going?"
So far so good. Then, nice thumbs up,
followed by walking into a lamp post.
Conk.

....

And it's thumbs UP.
Not thumbs SIDEWAYS.
And it's not middle finger up.
It's the THUMB.

....

After you give me the thumbs up, and
I return it, DON'T GIVE ME A THIRD
THUMBS UP, followed by an OK sign.
JUST WALK. Avoid lamppost.

....

....

Remember, you're a real person,
not King Lear. Don't orate the line.
IT'S UNREAL. No need to wear a giant
thumb. Wife started crying.

....

Anyway, LEARN YOUR LINES: Gee,
how many times did I hear, "How's the
screen-uh, thingy, whatever, whatsis,
line please! aw fergit it." Conk.

So frustrating when you have to text
but you're home so you have to go get
in the car and drive all the way to the left
lane of the freeway.

DOING CAMEO
ON CSI AS FACE
DOWN DEAD BODY
WITHOUT A CHALK
OUTLINE. WHY?
NEW EMMY
CATEGORY:
FACE DOWN DEAD
BODY WITHOUT A
CHALK OUTLINE.

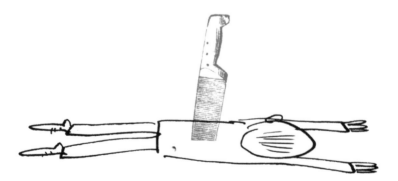

Rehearsing at home for tomorrow's CSI cameo, "face down dead body without a chalk outline." Maid screams.
Wife calls lawyer, then 911.

....

At the mall.
Think I'll do some rehearsing. Lie on sidewalk, get into "dead guy" character. Quite hard to do without chalk outline.

....

Did not go well at mall. Passerby said, "how's the screenplay goin', Steve?"
Worried about tomorrow's performance on CSI...and Emmy.

....

Driving home, trying "slumped over dead guy." No wonder this is Emmy stuff.

....

It's late. Need place to rehearse Dead Guy. I lie at bottom of stairs. Wife comes home.
Do I break character? Never.
She dials shrink.

....

Just did CSI cameo. Went well.
But got up, saw CHALK OUTLINE.
What? Miscommunication about role. EMMY
CHANGES DASHED.

....

CSI contrite. They've promised me a
shot at "man with briefcase" in final
episode. Working with briefcase now.
Have to flash briefcase brand. Hard.

Pretty hectic day. Got some letters in
the mail, now I'm busy alphabetizing them.
Back in touch tomorrow.

....

So great that alphabet already
in alphabetical order.
What a timesaver.

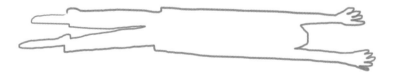

THIS IS AWFUL. SOMEONE HAS LEAKED MY CAR'S PRIVATE GPS LOCATIONS:

Current Location	Saved Location	Map

Home – 888 Muscular Bod Blvd

"Photography Studio"… Shed behind bushes, Culver City

Alec Baldwin Resentment Awareness Class – 9156 Avenue of the Stars

Little Waziristan – 1737-26 Warehouse Drive, Irvine

Frontier Hearing Aids & Dry Cell Battery Crotch Pouch Shop – 6 Casino Way, Reno

Academy of Motion Picture Arts & Sciences Ballot Stuffing Shadow Office – 8494 Wilshire

Helena's Big Wiener and Banjo Repalr – 41-10 Lankershim Blvd

L'Insole (Restaurant) – 3378 Santa Monica Blvd

Thong management lessons – 11502 Beach Road, Malibu

Whoretown – 290-703 Yorba Linda St

Ear Candlers Anonymous – St. Joseph's Church – 6632 Buena Vista

'Pouty lips' tutor – 11502 Beach Road, Malibu

Slippin' Sloppy Joe's Eggplant Sliders – 3882 Pico Blvd

Club Anxiety – 4777 Hollywood Blvd

Pete's Puppy Vanquishing Goodbye Farm – 625 Gladiola Circle, Thousand Oaks

Armani (Big Waist Store) – 5119 Discount Lot E

Money cave – Somewhere off 405???

The Museum of Crusty Stuff (TMoCS) – 95904 Sepulveda

Dr. Kissy-Cat Pickle Party (karaoke) – 6327 S Ardmore Ave

Tom Hanks prank-testing lab – 60010 Industrial Parkway, Glendale

Hair whitening – 2229 Mulholland Drive

More >>

It's odd.
No matter how much I keep eating,
I can't get my stomach to go flat.

Running low on Twitter feed.
Going to store to get more.

Now pretaping dog walk so I don't
have to take him out late at night.

I'm leaving town for two days
and I left the window to the right
of my front door unlocked.
I can't think of anything stupider.

. I leef driew yadot.

SING ALONGS

Around Christmas, I proposed sing-a-longs. (And this is where I first started collecting reply tweets.) I would "sing" the first line of a song, and followers would suggest the next word of the song:

**Now it's time to sing along.
I'll sing the first line,
and you'll sing the last words of that line!
DECK THE HALLS WITH ...?**

. . . .

Anonymous Tweeter: **Boutrous ghali?**

Anonymous Tweeter: **Salvador Dali?**

Anonymous Tweeter: **Buddy holly?**

Anonymous Tweeter: **Giant Otters?**

That's right,
"Deck the halls with Buddy Holly!"
Fa la la la la, la la la la
'Tis the season to be...?

Anonymous Tweeter: Stuart Smalley?

Anonymous Tweeter: Big and Tall-y?,

Anonymous Tweeter: Weezer?

Anonymous Tweeter: a Svengali?

Anonymous Tweeter: Smoking With Sir Walter Raleigh

Anonymous Tweeter: watching Along Came Polly?

Anonymous Tweeter: a border collie?

Anonymous Tweeter: **off your trolley?**

....

That's right,
"'Tis the season to be off your trolley,"
Fa la la la la, la la la la.
Don we now our gay...?

....

Anonymous Tweeter: **roommate Darrel?**

Anonymous Tweeter: **formal loungewear?**

Anonymous Tweeter: **Don we now our gay, I mean stylish, red sweater?**

That's right,
"Don we now our gay, I mean stylish,
red sweater," Fa la la la la, la la la la.
Troll the ancient...?

Anonymous Tweeter: green tinted cheddar?

That's right,
"Troll the ancient green tinted cheddar!"
Fa la la la la, la la LA LA!
It's been fun singing with you!
Xerry Christmas!

Okay, here we go. I'll sing the first verse,
and you sing the last few words: ♪

Rudolph, the red-nosed reindeer
had a very...?

. . . .

Anonymous Tweeter: **gaping wound?**

Anonymous Tweeter: **difficult Sudoku?**

Anonymous Tweeter: **large mortgage balloon
payment?**

Anonymous Tweeter: **inflamed nasal area?**

Anonymous Tweeter: **lucrative royalties deal with
clown costume manufacturers?**

························

That's right, "had a very large
mortgage balloon payment." ♪
And if you ever saw him...

························

Anonymous Tweeter: you would tell him he's
foreclosed?

························

And if you ever saw him,
"you would tell him he's foreclosed."

························

....

♪ All of the other reindeer
used to laugh and...?

....

Anonymous Tweeter: call some dames?

....

That's right, All of the other reindeer
"used to laugh and call some dames."
They never let poor Rudolph...

....

Anonymous Tweeter: join in any ponzi schemes?

....

That's right,
They never let poor Rudolph
"join in any ponzi schemes."

....

Then one foggy Christmas Eve,
Santa came to say:
"Rudolph with your nose so bright,

. . . .

Anonymous Tweeter: bring me Betty White tonight?

. . . .

That's right,
"bring me Betty White tonight!"
Then all the reindeer loved him as they
shouted out with glee...?

. . . .

Anonymous Tweeter: Rudolph the Red Nosed
Reindeer, you'll go down on anybody?

. . . .

That's right,
Rudolph the red-nosed reindeer,
if you're gay You can go into the
Armeeeeeeeeee! ♪

. . . .

*

Just when I think I have no more funny
tweets in me, I come up with this one.

A watched iPhone never syncs.

. . . .

My iPhone is now lip-syncing.

. . . .

iPhone just synced perfectly
with toaster. All is well.

. . . .

iPhone and computer heading off to
hotel spa for leisurely afternoon sync.
Back in 4 hours, they said.

....

iPhone and computer came back from
spa with DIFFERENT CONNECTOR
CORD. Is something going on?

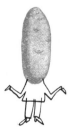

Trusting wife refusing to call me by my new
name, The Great Yam. Trouble at home.

....

Taking advice of Tweepster, I am
asking wife to call me The Galactic
Potato. She's refusing.

....

THIS IS A ONE
TIME ONLY
ANNOUNCEMENT:
IT IS 10:39 AM,
EASTERN TIME, ON
DECEMBER 19,
2010.

JURY DUTY

REPORT FROM JURY DUTY:
defendant looks like a murderer. GUILTY.
Waiting for opening remarks.

. . . .

REPORT FROM JURY DUTY:
guy I thought was up for murder turns
out to be defense attorney. I bet he
murdered someone anyway.

. . . .

REPORT FROM JURY DUTY:
Prosecuting attorney. Don't like
his accent. Serbian? Going with
INNOCENT. We're five minutes in.

. . . .

REPORT FROM JURY DUTY:
I'm cracking up defense with my
jokes. Judge not pleased. I like defense
attorney. Defendant finds me funny.
Nice guy!

. . . .

REPORT FROM JURY DUTY:
Other jurors are stupid. They don't
believe in "hexes." Plus, they want me
to put my magazines away.

. . . .

REPORT FROM JURY DUTY:
Defendant's hair looking very
Conan-y today. GUILTY.

REPORT FROM JURY DUTY:
Attorneys presenting "evidence."
Since when are security photos,
DNA, and testimony evidence?
Trusting intuition.

REPORT FROM JURY DUTY:
Now forcing my autograph
on other jurors. Also starting
whisper campaign of innocence
based on Magic 8 Ball.

Slipped into evidence blow-up of
fingerprint with my face worked into
it. Got screams! Judge now banging
gavel on my head. Hard to twee...

Defendant running for exit.
Not to escape, but out of disgust.
Judge wearing NOTHING
under his robes.

....

REPORT FROM JURY DUTY:
Finally, jurors are deliberating.
I'm bored, so I'm making a list
of my films in order of greatness.

....

REPORT FROM JURY DUTY:
Uh oh. Jury foreman mixed up verdict
with my greatest film list. Read out
three film titles and judge booed.

....

REPORT FROM JURY DUTY:
Defendant sentenced to death. Feeling
bad. Wait...call from REAL JURORS
OF BEVERLY HILLS. WORTH IT!

....

REPORT FROM JURY DUTY:
Sad about execution, since defendant
was proven to be at South Pole,
not Ralph Lauren Polo Shop
in Beverly Hills.

I am going on a diet for the next hour.

. . . .

Administering CPR to myself to recover from
hour-long diet. Drinking tea and sucking
on ice cubes made from bullion.

. . . .

Going on twenty minute
starvation diet.

. . . .

....

Satisfied with today's dieting.
Going to dinner now at Restaurant Row.
Not at one restaurant, entire restaurant row.

....

7 hour sleep diet worked great.
Will power held beautifully.

....

Weight now fluctuating wildly because of
twice daily 20 minute starvation diets.

....

Panic. Discovered bathroom scale resting
on Q-Tip for past 7 years. Off by 24 pounds.
Must lose it by New Years.

....

Going on 5 minute shower diet,
followed by 30 second tooth brushing diet.
They say these really work.

....

Next phase of weight loss program:
Brazilian Butt Workout. I've looked at a
hundred photos. So far, not working.

....

OMG (FYI, I abbreviated "Oh my God"
to save space [oh, I abbreviated "for your
information"], I made my own ten best people
list this year!

Two broken legs forces me
to cancel hokey-pokey dance recital.

. . . .

I can put right leg in, left leg in,
but hard to "turn myself around."
Which is, of course, what it's all about.

. . . .

. . . .

I put my right hand in,
then I shook it all about, then it fell off,
thanks to flesh-eating disease.

. . . .

With other hand, doing "pokey."
Still fun. Playing music LOUD.

. . . .

Now, what do I tell trusting wife?
That I was doing hokey-pokey
without her? This is not good.

. . . .

Been on the phone
for the last hour with hokey-pokey
anti-defamation society.
My official response forthcoming.

. . . .

I would like to apologize specifically
to the Okefenokee Karaoke
and Hokey-Pokey Dance Club
for any grief I may have caused them.

. . . .

....

Thoughtful Tweet upgrade:
If Socrates is a man, and all men
do the hokey-pokey, therefore,
that's what it's all about.

....

THIS JUST IN:
Scientists discover hokey-pokey
to be basic building block of matter.
So the hokey-pokey is, after all,
what it's all about.

....

@LadyAstronomer: **Where is this Hokey-Pokey
paper? Results need to be confirmed before
everybody "shakes it all about!"**

....

*NOTE: This is where I first started to save responders'
names and tweets.*

I have just been given
The "Golden Fellow Award."
This is a one-time award given out by me.
I'm suspicious of its validity, however.

. . . .

I have just determined that the
"Golden Fellow Award," given out by
me, is completely legitimate! NICE!
Prize came by FedEx I sent yesterday.

. . . .

I just pulled up in a limo at my own
house. Staff is taking photos of me
as I walk to front door.

I invented Facebook.
Lawsuit in preparation. Details to follow.

. . . .

My original site, GalPal,
morphed into Galrate, which became
GalPage, which was stolen by Al Gore.
Which became GorePage...

....

GorePage became GoreDiddy.
Which became DiddyBook. Diddybook
transformed into GalPal, my original site.

....

GalPal then became MisterGal, which became
FaceGal, which was stolen by Zuckerbook.
Copied by BookFook, then Oglegal. Which
became Google.

....

Google became Glee. Which became FaceGlee,
soon to become CuteKittenPhotos. Which, of
course, became Facebook.

I made a video for YouTube
but it went straight to the theatres.

Last night, watching show on my DVR.
Accidently saw three seconds of commercial.
Trusting wife stunned.
Dog hates me. Banned from remote.

. . . .

@Dark_Artz: You'll pull through champion.. this too
shall pass

@HitAndRunKitty: the proper word is
#telecommander.

@ADAMsauter: I let a whole series of commercials play
once. I live under the 405 now.

@Wtaussig: Can you still be called a man?

@dpalacio16: Did the dog quickly lift and turn his back
to glare at you then did a half muffled bark to show his
dissatisfaction?

SUPERBOWL

Buffalo wings = chicken wings in spicy sauce.
World = full of lies. : [

@PeterPoffles: **So how do buffalos fly then?**

@The_Iceman2288: **Hot dogs are worse, I was so disappointed when I found out.**

@TomR2D2: **Didn't you ever see Dances With Wolves? Using their wings to escape predators is the only reason they haven't gone extinct!**

@cheezmo: **French fries are actually potatoes and not fried frenchmen.**

I thought the "Ceremony of the Coin Toss" was incredibly moving this year.

. . . .

@ruffleader: **It touched me in ways that a priest never has.**

Commerciality is ruining
the Superbowl ads this year.

. . . .

@Reynoldsbon: I don't want to watch the
Superbowl till I read the book first. The show
leaves out all the characterization

@ShineALiteOnME: youre not funny at all.

@biffyb: Going through my contact list. Trying to
figure out who you are. Did you do the thing with
the one hour shirts?

(Attempting to class-up Tweets)
I think it was Oscar Wilde who said,
"Is it gay in here or is it just me?"

. . . .

(Attempting to class-up Tweets)
It was Charles Dickens who said,
"A Tale of Two Cities is a great title
for one of my novels, but which one?"

. . . .

@youcatastrophe: I think I'm the only person in
the world that truly understands you and gets
your humor. That said...you're not very funny

Conversed with shrink
about followers being funnier than me.
He really made me laugh.
Shrink funnier than I am.

On the street, ran into Bad, Bad,
Leroy Brown. So funny!
Funnier than old King Kong!

What's making me so hungry?
Is it the drive home from the restaurant?

THE OSCARS

Religious holidays notice: Oscars.
High holy week begins today.
Please respect my religion by not shooting
suction darts at your TV screen.

. . . .

@Violet_Davis: **Partaeeee POOPER!**

@mikesontour: **How about adhesive based projectiles? Is glue kosher?**

@zyblonius: **But real darts cause so much more damage.**

@DavisMets: **Too late.**

@Eden_Brower: **I worship at the church of the Teen Choice Awards.**

@1RoguePoet: **Crud, didn't even think to use suction... new screen required.**

@toqueguy: **In deference, I think that conflicts with the precepts and tenets of Nerf Wednesday.**

@bokonon07: **In OUR home, we reverently place our hands on the screen.**

@SherrieGG: Even over our shoulders with mirrors? Orthodoxy...

newbaby55: who will your God be wearing?

At 6pm PST, starting overnight caviar on toast-points fast, giving up capers and diced hard-boiled egg yolk condiments.

. . . .

@BorrisSpassky: Thank you for your suffering

Oscar Holy Monday:
The Ceremony of the Borrowing
of the Jewels.

. . . .

@howardweiser: **Are you making your way through the Stations of the Smorgasbord?**

@mdham_21: **what day is The Renting Of the Stretch Hummers ?**

@Donna_Ritchie: **Shouldn't have any trouble finding an ass to throw a cloak over.**

. . . .

Oscar Holy Wednesday:
The Coveting of the Nomination

. . . .

Oscar Holy Thursday:
The Holy Reading of Presenters'
Banter from Oscars Past.

. . . .

Oscar Holy Good
- But It's Just Not Right for Us - Friday

....

Oscar Holy Saturday:
The Sacrifice of the Virgins. Oh wait,
that takes place all through the year.

....

Oscar Holy Sunday Morning:
Today you are forbidden to
drive yourself.

....

Oscar Holy Sunday Afternoon:
The Holy Wedding of the Spanks.

....

Oscar Holy Sunday Evening:
The Holy Failure to Mention
One's Spouse.

....

There's a rumor that a recent Oscar
host is going to play Catwoman.
Waiting by my phone for the call.

....

@dougevil: I have dreamed of seeing you in the
leather catsuit.

@mattMICKenna: Oh no, Steve, that was Anne
Hathaway. I see why you're confused though. You
have hosted the Oscars.

@R_Optimist: I'd pay to see that ... well, on Netflix...

....

Doing a sit-up in preparation
for my Catwoman role.

....

@DorkinTWizzard: you might need to do two for
that role

@tralalajamie: work it boy

@flying_python: shouldn't you be licking your
paw and curling up in the sunshine?

. . . .

One sit-up has created ripples on abs.
Embarrassing when in tight tee,
with light hint of perspiration,
walking dog in bright sunlight.

. . . .

@pimplimpin: I know what you mean. Just
climbed flight of stairs and quads are chiseled.

. . . .

Preparing for Catwoman role by
leaping off roof into shrub. On third
try, I managed to hit the shrub.

. . . .

Trying to remember my Amazon password. Jerkone? Banjonut? Goofyguy? You-the-man? Speedowearer? Dang it! None work.

....

Thanks to your suggestions, have tried, Hatescans, Budgiesmuggler, Pepsicatflufferwoman, 92Y, w1ldnCr4zyg|_|y, Ol' Saggybag, AlwaysBeenGrey.
None worked.

....

Got it! Thanks to your reminders: HumbleStudMuffin

@Scriptking: **I'd have laid money on TutMeister.**

The colon is the world's shortest emoticon :

AKAMisterSmith: **does : mean Botox?**

I JUST
DOWNLOADED
ELEVEN HUNDRED
BOOKS ONTO MY
KINDLE, AND NOW
I CAN'T LIFT IT.

@comedy4cast: You should have downloaded the paperback versions. Much lighter.

@AshGhebranious: You mean I didn't need to buy a kindle for each book I downloaded????

@KeyboardHussy: Change the text size.

@urbanfish: I just read and responded to your tweet, and now I can't get that 45 seconds of my life back. Help!

@ChrisPerry0627: too funny. It made my mudd mask crack.

HI, I'M STEVE'S CAPS LOCK KEY AND I'D LIKE TO MEET OTHER CAPS LOCK KEYS. I'M INTERESTED IN BOATING AND HIKING.

. . . .

@pastelpastel: **I'M PASTEL'S CAPS LOCK KEY BUT AM VERY SHY. SO SOMETIMES i end up doing this.....**

@RaphPH: **your kind are not welcome here #lowercase**

@cam311: **HELLO CAPS LOCK KEY! DO YOU LIKE LOUD WALKS ON THE BEACH!?!?!?!?!?**

@jollroger1969: **Hi SCLk. I AM AN ELDERLY CAPLOCK KEY. I HAvE TROUBle keepING IT DOWn. need cApLOCK Viagra FOR MAINtaINiNG INTERfACE**

@jakefogelnest: NICE TO MEET YOU STEVE'S CAPS LOCK. I'M JAKE'S BUBBLE TEXT. SOMETIMES I FEEL LIKE AN OUTSIDER.

@allcapstweet: **SO NICE TO MEET YOU! I THINK WE WILL GET ALONG GREAT. I ENJOY VEGETABLE MASSAGE AND LLAMA TAUNTING.**

@DanaBrunetti: **Hello Steve's Cap key, I'm Dana's upside down key. I like hanging around mostly upside down.**

@AvivaVesna: **e.e. cumming's twitter account never had this problem.**

@itskatieanne: **@jakefogelnest: @SteveMartinToGo** "NICE TO MEET YOU STEVE'S CAPS LOCK. I'M JAKE'S BUBBLE TEXT. SOMETIMES I FEEL LIKE AN OUTSIDER." **ok WTF.**

....

i would like to apologize for the
behavior of my caps lock key.
i have slid a toothpick wedge under it.

....

From my window, I can see my
capslock key, boating.

....

@Diane_travelmom: Just to let you know, I tried
the slow-motion setting in my shower today, and
Wow! What a difference!

@allmytweets: doyouseemyspacebarintheboat?

Today's tweets are sponsored by
"Creepy Guy." Whenever you want
something done around the house,
be sure to hire "Creepy Guy."

@Sasha827: Hey, I saw that dude on match.com!

....

Creepy Guy here fixing basement.
Odd that he has to tie me up to do it.

....

Why is Creepy Guy doing exotic dance instead of repairing basement leak?

@gulsonroad: What if he's reading your tweets in the basement? "The tweets are coming from INSIDE the house!"

OH MY GOD! HI, I'M STEVE'S CAPSLOCK KEY. Not now you idiot. I'm dealing with Creepy Guy.

ARRGGGHHH! Just saw Creepy Guy charged for exotic dancing on his repair bill. Oh well. Later, Creepy Guy! Next week, roof repair!

I traveled across the country, but found Creepy Guy's green hammer in hotel bed. Eeww. Creepy.

Rare Bird Alert #3 on Amazon!
I'm as happy as a clam.
Wait. Are clams really happy?

. . . .

@gropious3: The chilling sound of clam-laughter
has caused many fishermen to quit the sea

Out on the town today.
I tried to tweet but couldn't find a tweet
booth. Maybe they're a thing of the past.

. . . .

@Heidi_vonM: And then when you find a tweet
booth you know its probably gonna be broken and
smell like pee inside :/

Found some great new twitter pants.
Tight red spandex with calf protectors.
I'm sure the quality of tweets
will improve now.

....

Added to twitter outfit. Got rubberized
day-glo vest that fits over nylon twitter
tee. Tweets sure to improve.

....

@xooglr: Unlikely to improve Twitter
performance unless you acquire matching latex
fingerless gloves and foam rubber orthotics.

@BuddyGott: I have the exact same twitter outfit.
Let's not wear them at the same place at the same
time, ok?

....

Tweet outfit complete. Wearing straw fedora with alpine feather and groovy mirrored wraparound sunglasses. Tweets sheer poetry now.

....

@Lineman1200: **Super sized rhinestone glasses to complete the picture. Please don't twicpic this. I'm trying to get over the ham image.**

Like in The Da Vinci Code, today's tweets will contain secret, hidden [YO MAMA] messages for you to try and discover.

....

@kansasbard: **Is it, "YO MAMA"?**

@DoesItMakeSound: **I suddenly have this desire to listen to Yo Yo Ma....**

@JDGDredd1050: **I must call my father's wife to get the next clue!**

@ClaudineDC: **Ooh. I can't wait for the first one...**

....

Another secret message is hidden in this [BANANAS ARE HIGH IN POTASSIUM] tweet.

....

@adimike55: **Do I need special glasses to see these messages. Do you sell them?**

@KaighLu: **Nope, still haven't found a single hidden message.**

@ProfeJMarie: **Dang it, is this one of those tweets you have to squint to see the cool picture? I can't ever see those. What IS it??**

@Terpsdude7: **but WHAT could it be... TO THE BATCAVE!**

Try to figure out what secret message
is hidden in this last tweet.
**[HINT: THE SECRET MESSAGE IS
"WHOA, HORSIE!!"]**

....

@Willhemina1R: **scared**

@redheadtech: **You're going to have to provide some
kind of decryption key. Your hidden messages elude me!**

@JohnSReardon: **did you get a medical marijuana
card recently?**

@Rickratt52: **Hope you will be well soon!**

@jscottwilson: **I will study this offline for a while.
Thanks Steve!**

@CharlieCurrie: **By you, do you mean me
specifically, because i am not sure I can live with
that kind of pressure?**

@dinofromnewark: I keep pouring lemon juice on my iPhone and I still can't read the secret message.

@tweetgajan: "Ha Ha I woose"

At home today, building a table.
I'm using data I found around the house.

. . . .

@cynicalife: good thing you didn't limit it to just the kitchen, then all you'd have are pie charts. Data tables are better.

Trusting wife angry at me for violating sacred pact of marriage. A married man, she claims, does not wear a bustle.

....

@tomgrasso: I gotta side with the Mrs. on this one Steve...

@bradhinshaw: It's still okay for unmarried men to wear bustles right? Right! I thought so. Thanks, Steve.

@SaraBuchan: well...not in the FRONT. That's probably what has made her angry. ;)

@KluvFM: Pssshhh If wearing a bustle is wrong then I don't want to be right.

@tell_me_why: Man, you had some detailed wedding vows...

Just saw a duck
in the shape of a cloud.

....

@Lord_Kayne: A shotgun will generally have that
effect at sufficiently close range.

Finally thinking about getting a computer.

....

@jamenta: You're going to need electricity to your house.

@droctopu5: Start slow with a standalone Pong game, then a Commodore 64, and so on.

@timdyson: Make sure it has an 'ANY' key for all those sites that say "hit any key to continue." Mine doesn't and it's so annoying.

@Jo_Crew: Why? Your handwritten tweets are so entertaining!

@DONCARRMAC: Two words, Trail Blazer. Or one word if you own a Chevy.

@grape73: The one you are thinking about getting is now obsolete. Please think about a newer one.

@Jaysunmoore: Gateway to microwaving.

Took Tylenol PM in the morning, and was arrested.

....

@RickLeclercq: I once took a shot of nyquil followed by a shot of dayquil. Nothing happened!

@JoeNewberry: I suppose it is only a matter of time before you are listening to AM radio at night...

I'm trying to incorporate more swearing
and abuse in my tweets, so why don't you all
go screw into things?

....

@DiamondMeadow: **How frickin dare you, you!**

@jessefuchs: **You're an assbutt.**

@MaggieJagger: **light bulb changed, what's next?**

@TBlack9JA: **hey stevey, how u screwing today??**

....

Love my new swearing, offensive, mode.
Going well around the house, too.
Did not know trusting wife
knew uppercut.

....

@mfaulk79: Wives surprise like that. I was
introduced to the flying armbar after testing out
your new policy in my home. Help!

@bhurt42: Wait until she demonstrates the Five
Point Palm Exploding Heart Technique.

....

Working on new stand-up act with just
swearing, no jokes. Feels right.

....

Combining good suggestions from
followers for lurid stand-up
breakthrough:
Jesum-crow, frickin fricky frick.

....

@sargent_bosco: **I think you should go olde tyme with consarn it, or rassafrackin.**

@NGUYENFAN: **don't forget "What the Front Door"**

@chelleannbella: **try sassafras? Like, kiss my sassafras. And goodness glaciers**

@kickingsnow: **serendipitydip**

@anothersecond: **what the muckel fucle are yoose talking about boy !**

@Bridgetknapek: **My favorites are Cheese and Rice and Holy Mostacholi**

@shugus: **I've also been partial to barn f'narkin.**

@shugus: **Sweet Haile Selassie!**

@Asintope: No nouveau swear fest is complete without the phrase "Scurvy Bar Nuns." Semantically null but sounds blasphemous as hell.

@ButchRenfroe: bender dabbin sloberdobin lollypop.

@CoolandClear1: sessin butts de frapoodle toodle boole de boogle - I do not know in which tongue I speak I think it is the mad one!

@malvernjon: no NSFW on your tweet. I read it in work. I feel debased. In other words, thank you :-) (you gin clutching sammle flange)

@BradKeene: You're crossing lines we didn't know existed.

Thanks to your suggestions,
am working ideal opening line to new
scurrilous stand up. Next tweet.

HELLO, MUCKEL FUCLES. I SEE
A LOT SCURVY BAR NUNS HERE
TONIGHT. SWEET HAILE SELASSIE,
BARN F'NARKIN, MILK-A-WHATS.
KISS MY SASSAFRAS.

REPORT FROM MASTERS GOLF:
Women not allowed as members because lack
of penis as can lead to dangerous imbalance
when descending stairs.

HANG ON
WHILE I KICK
THIS COCAINE
ADDICTION...

WOW, THIS IS
TAKING LONGER
THAN I THOUGHT...

OKAY, THERE.

BREAKING NEWS:
made a cell phone call today free of
oscillating, underwater sound.
I'll see if it is reflected on my bill.

....

@ambientgravy: ...WAIT... you're saying I can
make a call with this handheld tweeting machine?

@garyprc: that's going to cost you extra Dollar
meesta

@fallinlove93: Ha ha. Like that would ever
happen. You are such a funny man!

ADVICE FOR WRITERS

Advice for writers:
If you're a writer, a real writer,
a really, really real writer, like,
REALLY a writer, you should not write
a sentence like this one.

....

Advice for writers:
Always and thus be terse and
to the point, to the point, to the point.

....

Advice for writers:
Avoid using the word "unbeleebabull."

....

@RickNOKC60: Concur. That's as bad as "suposably".

@AuthorandPoet: unbeweebabaw wook it up

@CindyD1000: **oh-tay**

@tunester10: **I'm writing as we speak and ALMOST used that word. THANK YOU!!**

@Soulclaphands: **If not unbeleebabull, how about inconceebabull?**

@AlmightyEnigma: **good advice, like it much. Similar to coinkydink**

@urmyhappiness: **NOW you tell me. I cannabeelevit**

@dbfisokay: **thats my novel in the trash can**

@lizbethbennet: **Then how am I supposed to complete my Mike Tyson biopic?**

TWEET POKER

Illegal online tweet Poker:
I have a King, a Six, an Ace, a Club
and a Jack of deuces. I bet a dollar.

....

@JoshJack: I have a 4, 5, 7, jack, and a skip card
from UNO. I raise you a monopoly $20!

@REasson92: You sunk my battleship.

@MichaelScottJ: **FUCK THIS! You always fucking win! You dick, I am no longer ever playing with you.**

....

I fold my Ace, raise my King, card-wrench my club to a spade, twitch left little finger, back up to view cards, fall out window.

....

@VincentWaller72: **Make Vincent laugh**

@LAWGDOGG: **a joker, a 1 eyed jack, 11 of cups, a 3 of hearts from naked lady deck, raise 87 cents & hit me!**

@ChasetheShade: **tsk...Steve...<shakes head>..why.. did you 'back up..to view cards...You had 'em..man!**

@conan_o_brien: **Not cool, @SteveMartinToGo. I lost my wife in an Online Poker accident. RIP BunnyDancer47**

@tunester10: So I was going for a Sunday walk and out of nowhere Steve Martin falls on me with cards in his hands

@MrFingerbobs: Your buck and eight cents more you big baby.

Today is National Marijuana Day.
A day when...uh...wow,
Wolf Blitzer is SO funny.

Just bought sexy new body stocking.
In beige. With eyeholes.
Currently walking dog in neighborhood.
Tinfoil hat looks good, too.

....

@Italia_Federici: Copy cat

@AliceJane_92: **sexy ended at biege**

@thetrhoof: **great. . . but missing the wicker shoes**

@dvdmacd: **...did you ever stop to consider the dog in all this?**

Finally stopped all my junk faxes, but started getting junk Fed-Exes.

. . . .

@sarapomish: **I've been getting spammed by skywriters. I feel your pain.**

@_ChrisBallard: **watch out for the junk U-Haul**

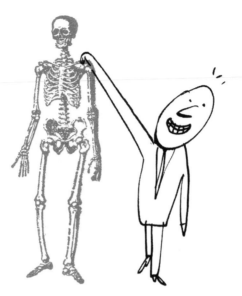

I have decided not to run for president.
Have skeleton in closet, which
is actual skeleton in actual closet.

....

@12SecondHorror: This is really a lot tamer than
most politicians' skeletons. You'd have a real shot
on the "I only killed a guy" platform.

Just bought a scythe. Hard inserting into scabbard in one smooth move, but must get it down for audition for "The ScytheMaster."

. . . .

@kevinstangle: and I will be Harvest Boy

@Nicronon: Lose a leg!... Um, I mean, BREAK a leg!

@johnstrand: glad to see that the less than stellar box office for The StairMaster didn't keep you from making a sequel!!

I like my antiques NEW.

. . . .

@RichCrossland: then you're a fan of face lifts.

FROM STEVE'S
COMPENDIUM
OF STRANGE
AND LITTLE
KNOWN FACTS:
THE BASKETS FOR
THE BASKETBALL
PLAYOFFS ARE
NOT WOVEN BY
NAVAJOS.

@QueenHelena78: **No fuckin' way.**

@SharonPCarr: **Reruns of F-Troop might dispute your findings of "fact".**

@vegassparkyrich: **What?!? Aw man....**

@PapaV: **Several of the baskets used by Navajos were, however, woven by members of the NBA.**

@NarrativeArtist: **Now I know who NOT to blame for these shitty baskets that don't hold anything!**

@KentCarlson1: **Great. Next you're going to tell us Eskimos don't make Eskimo Pies.**

@PapaV: **The NBA is also the #1 producer of knit socks among native nations.**

....

Idiotic scalpers in Lexington, KY have tickets
for my banjo show at $635.
I suggest you stick photo of me
on broom handle, play record.

I just finished finishing up
on a thing I was finishing.

. . . .

@Hetfield03: I do dee da chatchie.

@modenaboy: I just didn't do the thing I wasn't doing

From Steve's Book of Strange Facts:
As a reminder, the song,
"Dem Dry Bones" runs through orthopedic
surgeons' heads before operations.

. . . .

@zhandlen: Once woke up mid-surgery, heard doctor singing "The knee bone's connected to the--dammit. Dammit, dammit, DAMMIT."

The last thing bin Laden saw coming at him:

Bin Laden porn videos included
"I Can See Your Nose," and
"Is That a Toe I See."

@HIflyer: **Bin Laden favorite: "Girls Gone Outside"**

@64bitchrome: **he was into kinky stuff too, like "Girls Learning"**

@_chrisbrowning: **the lady with the plunging eye slit.**

Water falling from sky. Able to ward it off with magic blooming stick.

I'm wasting my time trying to come up with a good tweet, so, out of anger, I'm going to waste your time by having you read this one.

....

@majorflip: **I read it twice !**

@Anonnamus: **Joke's on you. I can't read.**

@Somos05: **Ha I didn't read it**

@Doreeski: **With all due respect: up yours Mr. Martin.**

@zackadamscomedy: **You win THIS round, Martin!**

**Decision to cut down use
of exclamation marks going great!!!!!
Discussions with college grammar professor
highly interesting!!!!!!**

**Can't decide if the word "awesome" even
needs an exclamation point. Answer: Yes!
It becomes even more awesome!!!!!**

....

@brad9778: **I think you were looking for awesomer.**

BAD DOG! (sometimes it helps if it comes from someone they've seen on TV)

. . . .

@QueenSlipstream: **OMG, you just made my cat do a ninja double kick with back flip shooter. Say something else and she may do the ironing**

@_Pohl: **great, my dog was really doing well in therapy... Now he thinks he's "BAD" again... MARTIN !!!**

Steve Martin admits to lying about.... It was on a beach in Florida.

A very good gardener I know just told me my
ass is grass. Nice compliment.

Brand new idea for making money:
Just copyrighted this word: the©.

....

@SusanL10: you'll make a killing on WTF's alone ;-)

@JasperSailfin: Where do I send the check? Oops,
there I go again.

@everlastinghigh: **Wow, you are a very smart man (HA! I don't owe you money for that sentence!)**

@dboii412: **the© stupidest thing ever. Oh crap it works**

@bigbeatottawa: **Clever, but I've found a way around le copyright.**

@JoshuaZehner: **Good luck on the©. My copyright on Himalaya-esk© has yielded surprisingly little. Considering doozy©.**

@JohnRBrewster: **I copyrighted "like©" and now own most teenage speech Now to just, like, get them a job and, like, make them, like, pay.**

@basementnoise: **Why stop there? Go for teh to, get the typo money too!**

Descartes owes me too:
I think, the©refore, I am.

@robtee2106: I thought he made maps

Thinking of moving to Alabama because
of ease of spelling the state.
Only four letters to remember.

....

@akmoss: It's why I moved to Oslo.

....

People are telling me Ohio only has
three letters to remember,
but I count five. O, H, I, HI, and HI-HO.
Please, get with the program.

....

@BlueLineTSCM: **Alabama=easy; kind of like** pointing to the food you want on a waffle house menu.

@Reynoldsbon: **How about Iowa? You probably** don't even realize you're saying the name of the state when you do a long yawn.

@wxlvr: **... Come on down, we'd be glad to have** you in Ablamala... Aw, crap....

@nhalejenkins: **i think you'd also have to spend** less time on personal grooming and learning.

@dandelions8910: **Also it's always first on those** pick your state drop down menus.

@e_phone_user: **only need 3 for Ohio. Save 33% off** Alabama.

@neiltwit: **And Alabama spelled backwards is** Alabama! Give or take.

@turner207: **Maine may not be the easiest to spell, but it's the fastest to say. That's also important.**

@robynl1230: **But the sequence! The darn tootin' sequence!**

Trying to get my new nickname to catch on: "The Elegant Argentinean."

. . . .

@thevastydeep: **Assume "Corky the Goat Herd" was taken?**

SOMEONE IS MOVING MY LIVING ROOM WINDOW AN INCH A DAY.

@primanirules: **around about cocktail hour**

@sailortweek: **It was ME. FOR SCIENCE.**

@TristanGemmill: **That'll be the precession of the equinoxes folk again**

@casinopete: **Its me. Now move mine**

@FrankSnotra: **@AlbertBrooks @SteveMartinToGo There's an asteroid supposed to hit Earth later 2night. You guys are movie stars-- DO SOMETHING!!**

@LancasterKat: **Do NOT read tweets from @stevemartintogo without first going pee! #dammit #justpeedalittle #sodamnfunny**

Tired of sitting on my butt.
Trying my shoulder.

Spent a lovely morning combing my lawn.

People love my earlier tweets.

. . . .

@Spectreman_71: **@albertbrooks I used to love reading tweets by @SteveMartinToGo Then he sold out and went mainstream around tweet number 437.**

@JacquesTheRippr: **You are far and away my third favorite comedy actor.**

@JessicaLuvsHS: **Fun Fact: I have the same birthday as Steve Martin. I'm cooler.**

BREAKING NEWS: NE WS.

I've decided I want to get to know Cher
on a first name basis.

Another beautiful day.
Wish I wasn't cooped up outside
on this dang boat.

. . . .

@CorenthalJames: **Wait a minute...that's silly.**
Now you're just being silly.

Haven't tweeted lately because I'm really
absorbed by a Bounty paper towel.

If you lean in real close,
this tweet smells of lavender.

Have just been diagnosed
with a borderline personality.

The secret of a happy life is [inaudible].

Loving my new facelift by Prada®.

Working on my new book,
"The Ten, Make That Nine, Habits of
Very Organized People. Make That Ten".

photo © Sandee Oliver

ABOUT THE AUTHOR

STEVE MARTIN IS A WRITER, ACTOR, MUSICIAN, AND performer. His film credits include *Father of the Bride, Parenthood, The Spanish Prisoner*, and *Bringing Down the House*, as well as *Roxanne, L.A. Story*, and *Bowfinger*, for which he also wrote the screenplays. He has won an Emmy for his television writing and Grammy awards both for comedy albums and for his work on the banjo. In addition to a play, *Picasso at the Lapin Agile*, he has written a bestselling collection of comic pieces, *Pure Drivel*; two bestselling children's books, *Late for School* and *The Alphabet from A to Y with Bonus Letter, Z!*; a bestselling novel, *An Object of Beauty*; and two bestselling novellas, *Shopgirl*, which was made into a movie, and *The Pleasure of My Company*. His work has appeared in the *New Yorker* and the *New York Times*. His album, *The Crow: New Songs for the Five-String Banjo*, won a Grammy for Best Bluegrass Album in 2010, and his current album, *Rare Bird Alert*, is nominated for a 2012 Grammy.

Steve Martin is contributing a portion of his royalties from this book to the Steve Martin Charitable Foundation which works with the arts and education.

This book was set with *Infidelity*,

an original serif typeface designed

by Matteo Bologna.